AF583659

In Memory of

Name *Address*

Name

Address

Name

Address

Name *Address*

Name	Address

Name Address

Name

Address

Name Address

Name | Address

Name

Address

Name

Address

Name

Address

Name Address

Name | Address

Name Address

Name

Address

Name

Address

Name	*Address*

Name

Address

Name *Address*

Name

Address

Name *Address*

Name

Address

Name

Address

Name Address

Name

Address

Name

Address

Name Address

Name

Address

Name

Address

Name

Address

Name

Address

Name *Address*

Name Address

Name	*Address*

Bereavement notices

Bereavement notices

Details of service

Details of service

Personal memories

Personal memories

Personal memories

Personal memories

Personal memories

Personal memories

Photographs

Photographs